*To all the socks I've lost over the years,
and to anybody who is feeling uncertain.*

Published by Stanchion Books, LLC

StanchionZine.com

Edited by Jeff Bogle

Cover art by Jeff Bogle

ISBN: 979-8-89292-684-3

THOUGHTS I LOST IN THE LAUNDRY

Leia Butler

STANCHION

Table of Contents

Sorry, just a few quick questions

How do I begin: Hello my name is Leia but everyone calls me Leah.

How do I begin: I'm 22 but I would rather be 40, or

How do I begin: I'm actually scared of the dark and I keep the door open a crack, with the hall light on.

How do I begin: When I'm asleep I can't quite believe the quiet.

How do I begin: She died 4 years ago and I haven't left those hospital chairs.

How do I begin: Smiling at 9am meetings when I can't feel a future.

How do I begin: Don't talk to me today, I am splintering by the seconds.

How do I begin: Pretending like I spent the weekend thinking about wallpaper paint instead of coffin colours.

How do I begin: Living when so much of me is just memory.

Red striped with the gold trim

They've always said fuck doesn't fit,
sounds wrong coming from my mouth.
I can never tell when someone is laughing or crying,
when their shoulders shake like birthday jelly,
red raw vibrations.
The update for today:
'I'm looking at an exciting world,
but I'm not living in it'.

8

So this is Monday morning

We are having our 'what I did on the weekend' chat,
the one where I say 'oh not much'
or nothing at all.

Linda is looking forward to lunch,
Fiona is worried about the wordle,
And I have questions of my own.

Like when is a 'quick chat' ever just 5 minutes?
or a 'how was your weekend' anything more than a formality
before a favour?
or how does time keep passing so fast,
and when will I catch up?

I am 72 in 50 years,
and I am worried about tomorrow's expired eggs,
and I do not have time to

each passing minute is calling me names,
because nobody ever said it to my face.

__Do you want to introduce yourself to the team?__

My name is: I am not ok.

Tomorrow: I might be gone.

Today: I am editing answers and eating a chocolate croissant.

Yesterday: I didn't think I'd see today.

In: 5 years I want to be failure.

Because: then I'll have a future.

It's not: nice to talk yourself into thinking you are tasting your last cup of tea.

You are: looking forward to Friday.

I don't: want to disappoint you.

I am: going to mute myself now.

Blue with a hole in the toe

The neighbour can see the glare of soap suds in my eyes,
she knows I have not been sending emails.

And like how she must catch me staring into her space,
sometimes, I catch her in mine.

Her, with her windows that she mops weekly,
real, clean, an extension of her external image.
Me, with my 15 tabs loading slower than the time it takes to boil
a bag of rice,
escaping to do another load of laundry when the washing
machine calls,
just treading water in between the digital despair.

How much a soul weighs

I watched a video that said a soul weighs around 21 grams,
about the size of a Freddo.
And I wonder what makes the weight?

Are we weighed by how often we do our 10,000 steps a day?
By taking the stairs more than the lifts?
By how many takeaways we have in a week?
By willingness?

Is a soul weighed by how much money we make?
Is a soul weighed by the colour of our nail varnish?
Is a soul weighed by the length of our commute to work?
Is a soul weighed by the light left in our bulbs?
By how many batteries you have laying around?
By how many bobby pins you've misplaced?
By stamps on loyalty coffee cards (including the ones you've
lost)?
Is the soul weighed by the lies you've told, collected up in
button jars?

Anyway, so how was your weekend?

Was this the thing that started it all?

We are talking about some of our first memories,
and they say things like 'my brother bit me!' or 'and I didn't
need the stabilisers after all!'
Everyone is laughing over 2pm tea and talk.

I am sitting on the bottom step,
toes smelling like lavender,
top sticking to a slightly wet back.

I can hear the crying,
between gulps, and screams, and questions.
I cannot see it.

There are 14 steps between us,
them, in the room that nobody will go in again,
us at the bottom, trying to hold hands over our ears.

And then the only other thing I remember
is coming home from school,
shaking strangers' hands,
dry and damp,
and I didn't know the details,
but my home had become a hole,
sandwiches and shells.

And I never saw him again,
and I lost her that day too.
And yes, I'll have a coffee please.

Shit did I leave the call while they were still speaking?

How long is one meant to smile and wave before pressing leave?
I've heard it's as long as it takes to boil the kettle,
Or 1 second for every 10 minutes the call lasted.

I am waiting for waiting.

If a meeting was a person, what would you rate them out of 10?

8.5 because they started the meeting late and your tea which was
the perfect temperature for the start of the meeting is now cold
7 because no agenda was sent and now nobody knows what this
meeting is
5.5 because only half showed up
4 because two people called you the wrong name twice
3.2 because it's scheduled over lunch and people are picking
salad leaves out of their teeth mid-meeting
2.7 because the 'you are on mute' tally is now over 10 and 4 of
those are from the same person
1.3 because your computer glitched and you only caught the end
of an aim or an objective
0.4 because you were only an optional invite and what happens
to the wasted hour and you could have been doing a laundry
load instead.

Pink with little love hearts

I often wonder if they are laughing at me,
sometimes I hear it outside my door,
so loud it feels like it's halfway in,
already taking off its shoes and saying we should put on the
kettle.

And a lightbulb in the lounge broke yesterday,
the end got stuck and we couldn't untwist it,
it said online we should use an onion as a quick fix.

But things break all the time.

Correct or not correct?

Correct or not correct, you can only think when it's loud?
When train wheels begin to whisper,
when you are only amongst strangers?

Correct or not correct, tomorrow you will be waiting?
For the coffee machine to finally be fixed,
for a feeling whether you really are quite the right fit after all,
for 12:05 to hit so you can pretend it's time for your packed
lunch,
for something else to drown you instead?

Correct or not correct, you have a list of coroners?
You know their first names,
and their favourite colours,
you are compiling a codex,
you are awake when you should be sleeping,
you forgot to press send on that email,
you can't wait not knowing what you are waiting for,
time is moving like mud?

Correct or not correct, you say nothing so you take up less
room?
You like facts over feelings,
you can't forget you once planned a future,
and your world isn't ending but it is getting smaller,
correct or not correct?

I am going through the spin cycle

I find myself in thought,
when the smile doesn't match the suit,
or the face the feeling.
When I've had one too many wines,
and the letters are melting in with the lights.
But I am just going through the spin cycle,
and it will all stop soon.

I'm just looking out of the window

It is at this time my Teams ticks me as 'away',
and that is fine,
I am making a tea,
or using the bathroom,
or

This is my mid morning:
snack or thrill or feeling,
11:35 is for making friends through reflections,

And maybe I made a mistake.

Blue ankle denim

What happens when they've forgotten my name 3 times in a
row?
Or forget they ever even met me?
I am smiling and sinking.

I was once taught that to make someone embarrassed,
is to kill them.

And I am deleting every tweet I type,
I am not laughing in case I have missed the meaning,
And I'm covering myself in crumbs,
a crunch coating to hide these habits.

You have a memory to look back on!

I have answered two emails today,
and I cannot answer any more until after lunch.

So my soup spoon is in one hand,
the other is cupped around my phone,
and I am expecting to see a celebrity baby,
a prank proposal,
I am expecting anything,
anything but my face staring back at me.

But it's not my face, it's my mother's.
And it's not my mother's either, she just has your face.

4 years and I see you again,
as a pop of pixelated pieces.
And it sinks me into my soup.

I click in closer.

You don't look like you aren't here,
you could be in the next room over,
playing online bingo and calling our names.

I click in closer.

I look at you, looking at me, looking like her,
a future frozen at 75,
just a memory to look back on.

It doesn't matter you don't know how to dunk a biscuit

Today we are taking personality quizzes before lunch,
and people are popping up us extroverts,
and they regularly make new friends,
and they can't wait to talk about their weekend,
and conversations are comfortable,
and I am standing in a room of strangers,
stringing along smiles instead of sentences.

Because I don't know the right way to dunk a custard cream,
and everyone is staring at me,
because I've been holding it too long,
and it is getting soggy with slight sweat,
and it falls into my tea with a splash,
and I blink,
and they carry on looking,
and I am crumbling too,
not knowing how to say how I am without,

and sometimes I can feel the words in my pocket,
caught between the inside lining,
and the tip of my tongue.

Typos after 10

I send messages with typos when it's past 10,
after after work drinks.

Knock knock,
I am a feeling,
I am 2:30 cup of tea,
I am chips,
I am did I leave my phone at work?

We are talking hinge dates,
the ones with dogs in their profiles,
or that answer the questions seriously,
we are worried that continuous swiping will lead to finger
fatigue.

You could do better,
I could do less,
why aren't we moving?
I can't quite tell you how I feel,

these are just moments.

Grey, blue dots, scallop edges

It is Saturday and I am consumed.
By sweat seeping into the sofa,
fusing with fabric,
by no excuse not to exercise today,
by the socks lined up on cold radiators,
towels crumpled in a corner,
by the fake feeling of free.

Because weekends are just weekdays with more chores.
And this month it feels like everything is running out,
and my drawers are filled with things I don't need
and it is time to put another load on,
using 38 quick wash to get through it all faster.

I like things better when they are wrong

Isn't it right you were the last one to hold her hand?
The next hands she felt were strangers?
You told her she was being silly?
You brought her jelly?

And isn't it right you told her she'd see you soon?
Do you think she believed you?
Do you think the words flew around in her brain like stirring
alphabet spaghetti soup?
Does it make you feel small?

Isn't it right they showed you diagrams of her heart?
Were you still hopeful at 50% chance of survival?
What about 30%?

Isn't it right that you thought you would make a difference?
As if you were a charm on a keychain?
And how much did you matter?

Isn't it right you felt numb when they broke the news?
The faces around you started to fly?

Why couldn't you cough out the words
to tell those who rang for updates?

You were still stuck in that last lie,
isn't that right?

FridayTakeaway54FloaTingF33ling22

Once every 3 weeks my computer makes me change my
password,
and every next Monday I forget what I changed it to.

I am scrambling for seconds like loose change,
and excitement is not orange and mango squash,
even if we go through half a bottle at a time,
and I don't have a ringtone, I rely on vibrations,
I am sewing up the holes in our socks.

Sometimes I think names as sirens stream through the windows,
curtains open a crack,
not because I am afraid of the dark,
but because I don't know how to say what I want people to
know,
and I'm just trying to paint a picture before I proceed.

Left or right foot

'Hello! How are you, it's been forever! Did I tell you I am delighted to announce, and I'm so pleased to be, and I'm honoured to have, and…'

/

Ask me again because you aren't really asking.

/

If you tap your left foot I'll answer anyway with:

I am delighted to announce, I'm throwing away broken pieces of a pint glass and taking out the rubbish on my lunch break

and I'm so pleased to be, counting friends by thinking about who will be around for a funeral

and I'm honoured to have been given a fear of feeling, and increased energy bills, and how is everything I own breaking at the same time? The world is getting worse all the time and I can't think about it or I'll never speak again and how on earth am I meant to remember about tomorrow's meeting when the grass is on fire because the planet is burning.

/

If you tap your right foot, I'll count backwards from 100 and slowly slip inside myself until you go away.

One blue polka dot, one pink little trees

I am matching missing socks this Sunday,
last minute laundry.
I've been trying to decipher a dream about my teeth falling out.
And saying something doesn't make it cement,
but it does make a memory,
and sometimes I turn a sock inside out in another,
so at least something holds a surprise.

Wednesday morning copy and paste

Is copying a crime,
if today I am emulating another image?
If I am not me, soup-stained pyjama shorts,
always afraid of being marked as away,
crossing fingers I won't have to speak this meeting?

If today I am a different person when I answer,
sharing screen to a different self,
I am two feet firm on the ground,
keep to a diary,
simple salad for lunch,
no sugar in my tea,
always wear a dress even WFH,
lipstick layered,
nails neatly plastered,
this is perfect, still in the plastic.

3 wine things

Tonight,
I am having a blinking contest with a piece of garlic bread,
it is soggy with butter,
it is saying all the right things,
it is better at Scrabble than me,
and the winner gets flowers on their grave.

Oh wonderful, a few minutes to think

We are being held at a red signal,
I am thinking about how the oven should've been preheated 10
minutes ago.

We are still at the signal.
The driver says we'll be on the move soon.
I am counting how many doors there are,
the exits are blocked by brick.

Tomorrow I have 5 meetings,
I will only be present for 3.
But there is a bank holiday on Monday,
a small celebration.

We can move once the train ahead has sorted its doors,
and the seconds are moving slowly.
In my mind, I unload the dishwasher,
I do not have a dishwasher,
but I might buy a bookcase soon.

The train is moving,
and my excuses melt away.
I set tomorrows 7:05am alarm,
And 7:06, and 7:10 and 7:15.
I pretend its 11:11 and I wish I were inside out,

Isn't that right?

Neon yellow with blue spots

We spoke baby names in the bath,
and I am building a tower of tea bags on the kitchen counter.

I've been riding the same train for 7 years and I still don't know
the platform names.
I predict them as I pass,
still surprised when I get it wrong,
and I don't answer the door without looking out of the window
first.

Did I really fall over if nobody saw?
Even if the fabric stuck to my knees,
and I had to peel it away like potatoes?

Sometimes I like lost things,
it reminds me there are still things to find.

Evening observations after after work drinks

I am sitting across from a mannequin playing crosswords.
His handkerchief says something is something
and we omit certain details.

3 wine train journeys go faster than one or four,
the buzz of being more,
than the one on mute who opens her mouth and swallows words.
And everyone saw but nobody asked,
those words get cooked in a pie at the end of the day,
mixed in with cream and missing meaning and frozen carrots.
You burn your fingers as you get it out the oven,
and promise to call your mother before nine.

And the stops fly past,
like you are deleting exclamation marks in emails,
swiftly and,
touching shoulders with strangers
doesn't feel like the worst you've done that day,
and now you are not the one who forgot the sugar in his tea,
or was so quiet they forgot you were still there,
you are 3 daredevil wines deep,
and in this moment in this train,
you feel you can finally unmute.

Those things that aren't real

I dreamt I met you last night,
tiny, and mine.
Not yet born,
but a promise of why it is better to believe.

But then my mole tried to run away from me,
and my boyfriend grew an extra pair of legs,

And things are never quite what they seem in a dream at
2:47am,
and the spider crawling towards my skeleton,
was just the corner of the bed.

Is your middle name Rachel or repetition?

Everyone had avocado for lunch.
I was the red amongst the green with microwave pasta.

They say taste buds change every 7 years, or you have to eat
something at least ten times before you learn to like it.

And I'm worried they'll ask me what else I like,
and the same spaghetti strands I eat 3 times a week will stay
stuck inside me,
and they'll see my knots and know,
they will pass notes saying, 'she missed her chance'.

But even so,
I am boiling a pot of pasta for tomorrow's lunch,
and I have resigned to the routine.

2 Adidas perfect pair navy

We liked donuts after 3:30,
sometimes a Vimto,
not coffee though,
not to our taste.

And now I am working 9-5,
and you like iced caramel coffees,
and we are not 14 and 12 anymore.

<u>And how are we all doing this morning?</u>

Hair? Unwashed.
Jumper? 3 days worn and smells of tomato soup.
I am not working hard,
or hardly working,
I am the floaty bits in my cup of tea that I sip when I don't know
the answer to, 'And how does this fit into the budget?'

I carry plasters in every pocket,
I like how they feel they can fix things,
even though I don't have the same middle name,
and I miss her every time I look in the mirror.

At lunch I jump in puddles looking for depth.
And why do I have to cook dinner when I really want to drip
down the drain?
She always told me I could do anything,
so why don't the days fly by faster,
why am I stuck between 3:45 and 4:52,
why was I late to work this morning when I work from home,
why can't people keep promises,
why couldn't I have said no with a bite,

I am just putting on a plaster.

The best part of the meeting

I have put myself on mute,
my home from home,
here, I am mostly me,
hidden honestly,
celebrating my silence,
drinking tea through my teeth.

A new layer please

Do you recall the first time you slid out of your skin?
It wasn't because you ran out of orange juice,
or your jeans shrunk two sizes in the wash,
or even that someone ate the last packet of crisps,

it was because this isn't the nightmare you blew out birthday
candles for.

White with yellow and green pineapples

Tonight is an anniversary.
Tonight I am ignoring.
Tonight the label on the bottle is ripping,
and I am not I am not I am not,
these are not the right wine vibes.
And how can I drink this in front of your face,
and you ask me if it tastes nice,
and how can I say no when you bought it for me,
and you are still smiling,
and I imagine your insides,
and this is handwash only.

Yes, but there are only 5 hours left...

Sometimes I fill the kettle over the max line,
when I've said yes to a question that didn't require an answer,
or when I respond to the wrong name,
and I drink the tea when I know it's too hot.

Sometimes I play games during my meetings,
like matching faces with fake futures,
or guessing what their next word will be,
and I feel better when I fail,
because this is just a moment.

What comes before hello?

Sorry!
Sorry,
Sorry.
This is a sorry with a smile.
This is a sorry before hello.
This is an instinct.
This is breathing in and breathing out.
This is the second part to the question first.
This is my security.
This is my shame.

It leaves my lips before I can catch it,
like when you pick up a piece of toast,
not even bite it yet,
but now you have to get out the Hoover.
And I am forever sweeping away the sorries,
find and replace,
I thought I could control them if they were just words.

WFH 4 out of 5 days

One day a week Wednesday after work drinks are for bonding,
for separating the professional from the person but with wine.

You know you've got this morning's breakfast bowl to wash up,
and the soup is sitting in the fridge getting closer to its sell by
date,
but here you are talking about what it means to work past 6,
tearing apart your salaries like lettuce leaves in a salad,
and it's time for another cocktail,
for something different on the feed,
and you store these conversations in biscuit tins,
and tomorrow when life locks you again,
when you are back to nice top, pyjama bottoms,
prepping dinner in your lunch hour,
scrubbing at stains on the hob,
you'll replay these moments,
confused at what character you are playing today,
wondering if all you are doing is just wasting.

White fluffy reindeers

And the cold brings consideration,
a re-evaluation of resolutions,
like 'should I try actually eating my 5 a day?'
or 'maybe I am spending too much time on TikTok'
and it's too easy to get lost in other's lives,
so you finish off the fizz before it gets flat,
and write on the back of chocolate wrappers

Something like:
I want to exist in "well..."
that second half of the sentence,
Because worse than dying would be to die without the dot dot
dot,
the bit of the thought that bites,
an inside joke,
or a promise of 'I'm not actually invisible'.

All the unfinished things

A packet of Haribos, there are 3 cherries left.
15 notebooks (10 completely blank, 3 with only the last page filled).
My 10am tea.
3 tins of Vaseline.
The ironing.
5 pictures she'd been meaning to frame.
The payments on the 3 seater.
The Star Wars Trilogy.
My 12pm tea.
 1/2 the cake she was saving for when she got home from hospital.
The Christmas chocolates, mainly Bounties.
My 2pm tea.
A book she'd been reading 1 page a day for 5 years.
Sandwich crusts and crumbs.
3 emails half written in the drafts folder.
 The explanation for why exactly she died.
My 4pm tea.
£3.75 in change from a £5 note.
The story about why she collected duck figurines.

But yes, all on track for this week.

Almost at the top

Okay so it's Wednesday work from the office,
and I forget every other week that I'm actually afraid of
escalators.

I stand still,
hand clasped around the edge,
imagining I am just lying in bed,
and the baby downstairs is crying,
and cars are flying past outside,
and I am counting odd socks instead of sheep,
and the alarm will go off in 5 hours 33 minutes,
and the building I am falling off isn't real.

47

Where do all the sorries go?

When was the last time you heard a sincere sorry,
one gifted to you heavy in your hands,
not an 'oh sorry would you mind working late today'
or a 'sorry I forgot you were still there'.
And did you want to freeze it,
because sometimes it does not feel better to give,
you want to hold on to this one,
reheat it and serve it up in a soup,
bite into it and feel it burst against your cheek,
steam seeping,
swirling in your mouth,

and today is the first time my face looks older,
there are wrinkles under my eyes,
inside them are the sorries I've saved,
wrapped in tissue paper,
the ones that said something,
the ones that didn't shrink in the wash.

Socks I lost in the laundry:

Red striped with the gold trim
Blue with a hole in the toe
Pink with little love hearts
Blue ankle denim
Grey, blue dots, scallop edges
One blue polka dot, one pink little trees
Neon yellow with blue spots
2 Adidas perfect pair navy
White with yellow and green pineapples
White fluffy reindeers

About the Author

Leia is a writer from London. Her debut collection, *Tear and Share*, was released with Broken Sleep Books in August 2021. She is proud to have been recently published by Cutbow Quarterly, Roi Fainéant Press, Acropolis, and Streetcake. You can find her on X @leiabellebutler or via her website leiabutler.com/

Acknowledgements

A big thanks to Jeff for publishing this book and being such a joy to work with. This book is lucky to have a home with someone who cares so deeply about people and about the process of creation.

Thank you to Streetcake Magazine for publishing *Do you want to introduce yourself to the team?* and to Acropolis Journal for publishing *White with yellow and green pineapples.*

Thank you to my wonderful friends, family and everyone who inspires me.

And lastly, thank you for reading this book. If you have felt or are feeling any of the things explored in this book, know that you are certainly not alone.

ALSO AVAILABLE FROM STANCHION BOOKS

The Woman's Part by Jo Gatford

The House of Skin by Karina Lickorish Quinn

Where We Set Our Easel by Mandira Pattnaik

Irregulars by Kerry Trautman

It Skips A Generation by Alison Lubar

Ghost Mom by T Guzman

The Unaccounted for Circles of Hell by Lynne Schmidt

UNTENABLE MYSTIC CHARM by travis l. tate

We Don't Know That This Is Temporary
by Adrienne Maria Barrios

My Dungeon Love Affair by Stephanie Parent

Learn more at StanchionZine.com

Milton Keynes UK
Ingram Content Group UK Ltd.
UKHW041724260324
440099UK00004B/95

9 798892 926843